10/29/01

DATE DUE

NOV 1 4 2001			
Nov 29, 2001			
DEC 1 4 2001			
DEC 2 9 2001			
FEB 1 1 2002			
JAN 1 1 2002			
FEB 3 1 2002			
OCT 1 4 2002			
FEB 1 9 2003			
OCT 2 7 2004			
MAR 0 6 2007			
MAY 0 9 2009			
JUL 3 0 2009			
DEC 0 8 2010			

I want to be a Truck Driver

I WANT TO BE A

Truck Driver

DAN LIEBMAN

FIREFLY BOOKS

A FIREFLY BOOK

J 388.32 LIE

Published by Firefly Books Ltd. 2001

First Printing

Canadian Cataloguing in Publication Data

Liebman, Daniel
  I want to be a truck driver

ISBN 1-55209-576-2 (bound)   ISBN 1-55209-574-6 (pbk.)

1. Truck drivers – Juvenile literature.   I. Title

HD8039.M795L53 2001   j388.3'24   C00-932620-0

U.S.   Cataloging-in-Publication Data
(Library of Congress Standards)

Liebman, Daniel
  I want to be a truck driver / Dan Liebman. —1st ed.

[24] p. : col. ill. ; 20 cm. –(I want to be)
Summary : Photos and easy-to-read text describe the job of a truck driver.
ISBN 1-55209-576-2 (bound)
ISBN 1-55209-574-6 (pbk.)
1. Truckers – Vocational guidance. 2. Occupations
I. Title. II. Series
388.32/ 023 21   2001   AC   CIP

Published in Canada in 2001 by
Firefly Books Ltd.
3680 Victoria Park Avenue
Willowdale, Ontario, Canada
M2H 3K1

Published in the United States in 2001 by
Firefly Books (U.S.) Inc.
P.O. Box 1338, Ellicott Station
Buffalo, New York, USA
14205

Photo Credits

© First Light/W. Hodges, front cover
© Bette S. Garber/Highway Images, pages 5, 6, 16-19, 22-24
© Masterfile/Dale Wilson, page 7, back cover
© Masterfile/Roy Ooms, pages 8-9
© Masterfile/Mark Tomalty, page 10

©Chuck Keeler, Jr./The Stock Market, page 11
© CORBIS/Walter Hodges, page 12
© Sherman Hines/Masterfile, page 13
© Lloyd Sutton/Masterfile, pages 14-15
© Al Harvey, page 20
© Andrew McKim/Masterfile, page 21

Design by Interrobang Graphic Design Inc.
Printed and bound in Canada by Friesens, Altona, Manitoba

The Publisher acknowledges the financial support of the Government of Canada through the Book Publishing Industry Development Program for its publishing activities.

Being a trucker means more than just driving. You also have to check your fuel and look after your truck.

Big trucks are called tractor-trailers. The driver sits in the powerful tractor that pulls the heavy trailer.

The driver is proud of his shiny tanker. Tankers are used to carry milk and other liquids.

After this driver empties his dump truck, he will go back and pick up another load.

Some truckers drive at night instead of driving during the day.

Truck drivers must be prepared to drive through heavy snow in winter.

If there's an accident, drivers use CB radios and telephones to call for help.

Keeping records is an important part of a truck driver's job.

After having their truck weighed,
drivers can have a meal.

This husband-and-wife team drive the truck. At the end of the day, they prepare a meal in the tractor.

Truckers pick up their cargo at interesting places. This driver is loading up at a shipyard.

Drivers enjoy their work and are proud of their vehicles. Sometimes a driver will even dress up a truck and show it off.